P9-DUO-935

Itasca Realty
GMAC ™
Real Estate

E-mail: itasca@uslink.net
218-326-3411
Toll Free 1-888-326-3411   www.itascarealtygmac.com

Service You Deserve
People You Trust.

GRAND RAPIDS & ITASCA COUNTY
Looking Back ~ The Early Years
A PICTORIAL HISTORY

PRESENTED BY THE HERALD-REVIEW AND THE ITASCA COUNTY HISTORICAL SOCIETY

Table of Contents

Foreword

Itasca County is located in about the center of the northern half of the state of Minnesota. We are a land of forests, iron mines, farms, towns and villages, vacation resorts and summer homes.

Timber and mining played the biggest role in the early settlement of our communities. Most important to the charm of Itasca County are the hundreds of clear lakes that lie thick in its central section and are scattered almost everywhere else as well.

We were fortunate that people in Itasca County brought to us their picture stories and we are now able to share them with you. All of these photographs are part of the Itasca County Historical Society collection housed in our Karjala Research Center. We hope you'll sit back and enjoy this book and share it with your family and friends.

Thanks to Brian Vroman, Itasca County Historical Society research assistant, for writing the introductions to the segments of this book, the Grand Rapids *Herald Review* who saw a vision for this first book in the series, also to Bill Adams from Pediment Publishing for taking the time to visit with us and capture a picture of times past.

We look forward to the next book.

Lilah J. Crowe
Executive Director
Itasca County Historical Society

Scenes

Originally comprising much of northeastern Minnesota, Itasca County was one of the last regions in the continental United States to be settled.

Early photographs depict Itasca's rugged beginnings. Rough logging and mining towns were characterized by dirt streets and simple wood-framed buildings.

Yet, even in the early days, forward-looking community leaders envisioned an Itasca County more suitable to family life. A prime example can be found in the 1895 erection of Central School in Grand Rapids. Built at a time when logging was on the decline and the paper mill was several years in the future, Central School demonstrated the resolve of citizens for whom Itasca County was home. Similar tenacity was exhibited by residents of other Itasca communities.

The scenes in the first section of this book are indicative of Itasca County's rustic early days.

The steamboat "Irene" on the Mississippi River near the Itasca County Courthouse, 1902. The "Irene" is on its first Mississippi trip from Aitkin to Grand Rapids.

Cohasset street scene, circa 1905.

An early view of Coleraine.

Deer River, 1905.

An early view of Grand Rapids with the courthouse on the right.

Prairie River Dam, circa 1910.

Grand Rapids, 1899.

The town of Keewatin, circa 1910.

Aerial view of Keewatin with the mine on the right, circa 1910.

Nashwauk Main Street, October 25, 1903.

Oliver Iron Mining Co. buildings and homes for employees in Marble, October 15, 1908.

King Lumber Co. and Grand Rapids residences, circa 1910.

Main Street, Grand Rapids, circa 1912.

Birdseye view of Grand Rapids, 1940.

Gathering along the street in front of the Itasca Dry Goods Company and post office, 1913.

Looking south on Pokegama Avenue in Grand Rapids, circa 1912.

Logging

Logging played a crucial role in Itasca County history. In the latter decades of the 19th century, logging companies, attracted by seemingly endless stands of virgin White Pine, began operations in Itasca County.

One of the first areas where the ring of the axe was heard was the pristine Pokegama Lake region, where majestic forests reached nearly to the water's edge.

Logging was done primarily in the wintertime, when it was possible to skid fallen trees out of the forest on ice roads constructed for the purpose. In the spring, logs were driven down river to sawmills at points south. Highly skilled lumberjacks kept the logs from jamming.

Early lumberjacks were a breed apart. Rugged and hardy, they were able to endure the most demanding work in a very inhospitable climate. Sometimes colorful and flamboyant, lumberjacks developed their own unique "macho" culture. When not in the logging camps, favorite activities included drinking and fighting.

Prize load of logs from Taft Camp, 1902.

Logging on King Lake, 1892.

C.M. Erskine Timber Co.'s log drive on Prairie River Falls, circa 1900.

Logging crew in Itasca County, circa 1900. William Jones is the man on the far left.

Loading logs near Grand Rapids by the regular means of a chain and rollers. Power is furnished by a team of horses. Ron Hylla is the loader standing in the center foreground.

Sawing logs, circa 1900. The Milaney home is in the background.

Loggers in Itasca County felling a tree, circa 1900.

Steam log hauler used at Swan River Camp, circa 1900. The machine was built by F.S. Farr of Akeley Lumber Co.

Itasca County logging camp, circa 1900.

Team with a load of logs, circa 1900.

John Fraser Camp No. 1, 1902. George Arscott served as cook, Carl Eiler as the clerk.

Pulling a load of logs from Itasca County woods, circa 1900.

Stables at the George Arscott logging camp, 1906.

Meal time at a logging camp, circa 1905.

Loggers at an Itasca County logging camp, circa 1905.

Joe Gauvreau and Axel Morencey logging at the Skelly Bros. Camp at Spring Lake, January 15, 1907. The temperature was 35 degrees below zero that day.

Logging camp near Bovey, circa 1908.

This steam hauler, owned by the Joseph Gibson Co., Deer River, hauled 18 million feet of logs in 1909 from January 1 to March 1.

In the logging camp kitchen, Bluntach and Mitchell, Bovey, circa 1905.

Men and women perched on a pile of logs, circa 1910.

Logging camp between Bovey and Taconite, 1909.

Raising dead heads on the Mississippi, circa 1910.

Camp office at Connors Camp, 1916. From left to right are: Davis, Connors, and Hachey.

Bert Munson's Logging Camp four miles north of Taconite, 1915. Included are: Larke Huntley, Hugh McKewan, and Frank Sherman. The camp's cook was "Scarface" Riley.

A full load leaving the logging site, circa 1920.

Industry & Mining

With the decline of logging, Grand Rapids desperately needed a new economic base.

After exploring various dead-ends, a group of Wisconsin investors provided backing for the construction of a paper mill. In 1902, the Itasca Paper Company (later purchased by Charles K. Blandin in 1916) produced its first sheet of paper. The paper industry remains to this day a vital part of Itasca County's economy.

Meanwhile, mining operations were beginning on the Mesabi Iron Range. In 1905, the Oliver Iron Mining Company tasked former Rough-Rider and noted Yale athlete John C. Greenway with opening the western Mesabi and developing a technique for the use of its sandy ore. Greenway was successful, and for decades, iron mining rivaled paper making as the most important Itasca County industry.

Shingle mill at the Grand Rapids paper mill, 1908.

An early Itasca County blacksmith shop.

George Booth's cigar shop, Grand Rapids, 1894. Strippers were Bill Hennesy and Roy Lathrop.

Itasca Paper Co., 1902. The business later became the Blandin Paper Co.

Track gang for Hawkins Mine, Nashwauk, 1902.

Charles Johnson blacksmith shop, Hawkins Mine, Nashwauk, circa 1900.

Crosby Mine, Nashwauk, circa 1904.

Canisteo Mine near Bovey, circa 1900.

Ore washing plant near Bovey, circa 1905.

Steam shovel at Hawkins Mine near Nashwauk, 1902.

First trainload of ore taken from the Canisteo pit, July 29, 1909. The ore is being loaded by Alphonse Beaudet, operating Shovel No. 1346. H.F. Downing is standing by.

Oliver Iron Mining Co. train leaves the Canisteo Mine, 1907. Ernest Winbert was the engineer; August Lexen was the fireman.

Machine shop at Hill Mine, Calumet, fall 1908.

Mining the Walker pit near Calumet, spring of 1908. Jimmy O'Hern was the shovel operator, Mark Nagel the cranesman, and Ernest Wenberg the fireman.

Open pit iron mining by the Oliver Iron Mining Co., Coleraine, 1906.

Crew that constructed the Hawkins washing plant near Nashwauk for the International Harvester Co., circa 1912. Matt Rantala is one of the crew.

Drilling equipment used to look for iron ore, circa 1909.

Steam shovel at work in the Judd pit at Taconite, 1912.

Construction started in 1906 on the first washing plant for iron ore in Trout Lake Township. Six carpenters maintained the crude building and its equipment for the Oliver Iron Mining division.

Grand Rapids paper mill, 1908.

Workmen making "heads" for wooden barrels at the Itasca Paper Co., 1908.

First threshing machine in Wawina, 1906. George Unje, the owner, is standing on the machine.

First self binder in Bear River and Togo, circa 1910. The machine was owned by Gilbert Lee of Bear River.

Sawmill at Warba, 1910.

Grand Rapids paper mill, circa 1910.

Interior of Grand Rapids paper mill, circa 1910.

Mining camp at Bennett Mine, Keewatin, 1910.

Foremen and office force at the Hill Mine, Marble, 1911.

Machine shops at Hill Mine,
Calumet, circa 1910.

Survey crew for Hill Mine, Marble, circa 1910.

Itasca Co-op Creamery, circa 1910.

Mining in Itasca County in its heyday, circa 1920.

Louie Roeder, Fred Seckinger, John Benton, Joe Fremont, and Harry Skyberg working bare-footed in the papermill, 1913.

Working the mines, circa 1920.

Paper making at Blandin Paper Co., circa 1920. This was the Number Three machine.

Rail siding and track crane loading logs in the wood yard at Blandin Paper Co., circa 1930.

Commerce

In 1872 Itasca County's first store, a general merchandise store, was established on the site that would become Grand Rapids.

Business was brisk from the beginning, fueled by the seventeen lumber camps operating within a few miles of Pokegama Falls.

In those early days, whenever a settlement was started, about the first buildings erected were log structures where liquor was sold, meals were served, and where a lumberjack could get overnight accommodations.

Soon the log structures gave way to more substantial and permanent businesses, such as the Pokegama and Gladstone hotels.

By the turn of the twentieth century, the main streets of communities throughout Itasca County were lined with merchants providing the goods and services for the growing area.

The downtowns we know today were shaped in those years.

John Beckfelt's store and Lumbermen's Bank, Grand Rapids, circa 1892.

Potter and Casey Hotel, Grand Rapids, in the early 1870s.

John Beckfelt's first store and post office, Grand Rapids, March 2, 1889. Beckfelt is standing on the step.

L.F. Knox store on the corner of 1st Street and Leland Avenue, Grand Rapids, 1889.

Itasca Mercantile Company, circa 1898.

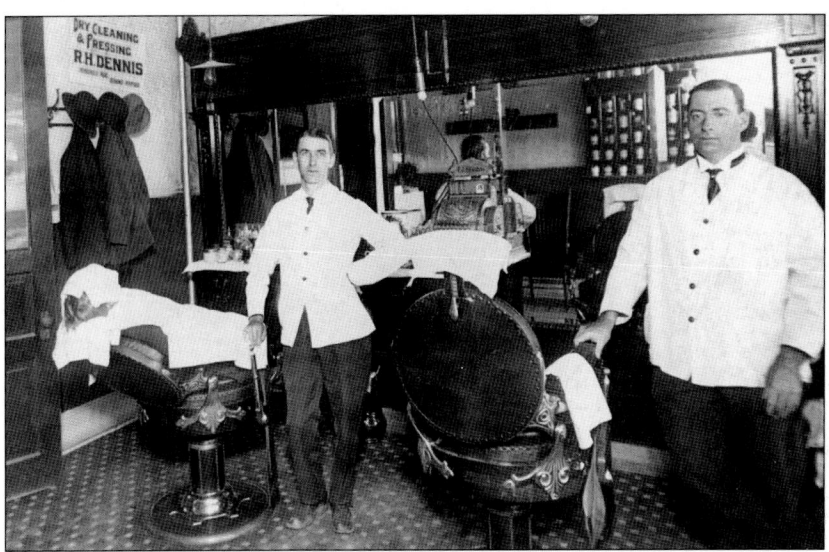

Pete Billeadeau, left, in his barbership, circa 1900.

Kennedy Hotel, LaPrairie, circa 1900.

Wright Mercantile Co. store and post office at LaPrairie, circa 1900.

Joseph LaFond's barbershop, Grand Rapids, circa 1900.

The Stevens Hotel also housed a confectionery in 1892.

Pokegama Hotel lobby, circa 1900.

Pokegama Hotel bar, circa 1900.

Metzger Bros. Meat Market decorated for the Christmas season, circa 1900. The three brothers are, starting with the second man from the left: Charles, Bill, and Tony.

A Grand Rapids millinery, circa 1900.

Hotel Pokegama, Grand Rapids, circa 1897.

An Itasca County saloon, circa 1900.

Henry Hughes store, Grand Rapids, circa 1900.

Henry Hughes store at the turn of the century.

Grand Rapids grocery store early in the century.

Grand Rapids grocery at the turn of the century. From left to right are: Ed Gates, C. Glover, Felix Signel, and Lander Larson.

George Wilson livery barn in Coleraine, 1910.

Gunar Smith store, Grand Rapids, circa 1910.

Shannon's Sale and Dray Line barn and veterinary office, Grand Rapids, circa 1910.

First boarding house in Nashwauk, Saari Koski, circa 1906.

Livery Stable run by Doc Parmeter in Deer River, 1908.

Itasca Dry Goods store, Grand Rapids, circa 1910.

Ogema Hotel stood on the banks of Pokegama Lake. Built in 1904, it was the site of the first golf course in the area. It was destroyed by fire in 1928.

Sam Patterly saloon, 3rd Street West, Grand Rapids, 1909. The man second from the right is Ed Cloutier.

Moving the Roan Hotel, Bovey, 1910.

Oliver Mercantile, Taconite, circa 1900. Robert Loux was the proprietor. Also pictured are David Roche, meat cutter; Lucy Burns; and Margaret Burns, Postmistress.

Grace Fraser is the clerk in this Grand Rapids store, circa 1910, which sells, among other things, woolen underwear.

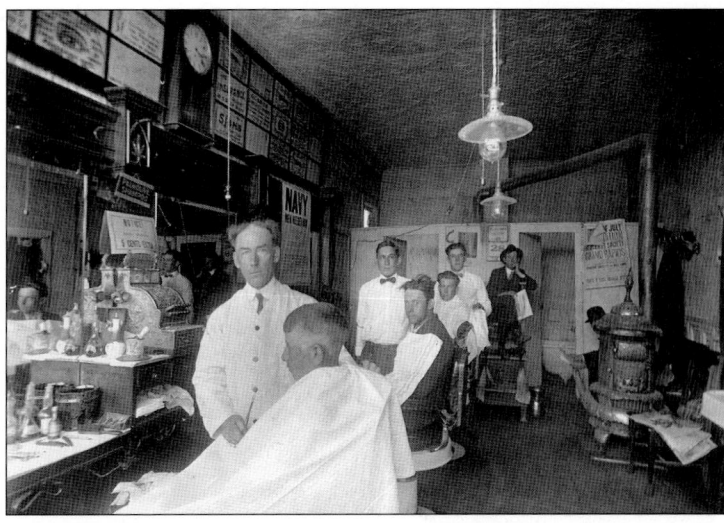

Joe O'Day's barbershop, circa 1910. The barbers, front to back, are: Joe O'Day, Louie Bouvette, and E. Wardell.

Tellin Store in Deer River, 1912. Shown here are Mr. and Mrs. Tellin, William Hawley, and Ida Gellerman.

Dolly's Restaurant, Grand Rapids, in 1917. The women, from left to right, are: Dolly Powell, Marie Powell, and Mrs. Alex Hachey.

Itasca Mercantile Co. grocery department, 1911. Salesmen behind the counter are Jim Connell, left, and Leonard "Porky" Blanchard, right.

Henry Hughes store, 1911.

Billeadeaux's restaurant, Grand Rapids, 1912.

Office in the Beckfelt store, 1912. The woman is Jennie Frank.

Interior of a Grand Rapids business with Louis Schugel, Mrs. John Craig, and John McKeown.

Skala grocery store, Keewatin, 1920. Pictured are: Louie Defonso, delivery boy and salesman; Andy Olson, butcher; Jake Skala, the owner; and an unknown man.

Shoe and harness repair shop of William Neumann, Sr., Grand Rapids, 1916. It was housed in the John Beckfelt building and the sign out front read I.C.D.A. William's 16-year-old son, Walter, is waiting on an unknown customer.

Peterson-Dimatteo store, Calumet, 1919. John Steinberg is the meat cutter; Hilding Peterson is on the left.

C.F. Tellin Meat Market, Deer River, circa 1920. C.F. Tellin is standing directly behind the driver of the tractor. Howard Kiehl Tellin is the small boy standing on the wagon tongue. Kenneth Noel Tellin is standing directly behind Howard. The family lived in the upper left of this building. Mr. and Mrs. Binder had a bakery on the lower left. The meat market is in the middle. Nell Hawkins, Tellin's sister, lived in the lower right with children Lewellen, Ida, and Gladys.

The Unique Theatre owned by Crocket Brown, Nashwauk. A silent movie, "Social Code", made in 1923 and starring Viola Dana, was showing.

Achesons Tire & Battery Service, 1923. Ed Person's machine shop is on the left. Nick Kines had a tin and metal shop on the right where he made toboggans for Don Acheson. Acheson's building was formerly the Odd Fellows Hall and meeting place of the Ku Klux Klan.

The Royal Bar and The Rapids Cleaners, Gilboe, circa 1940.

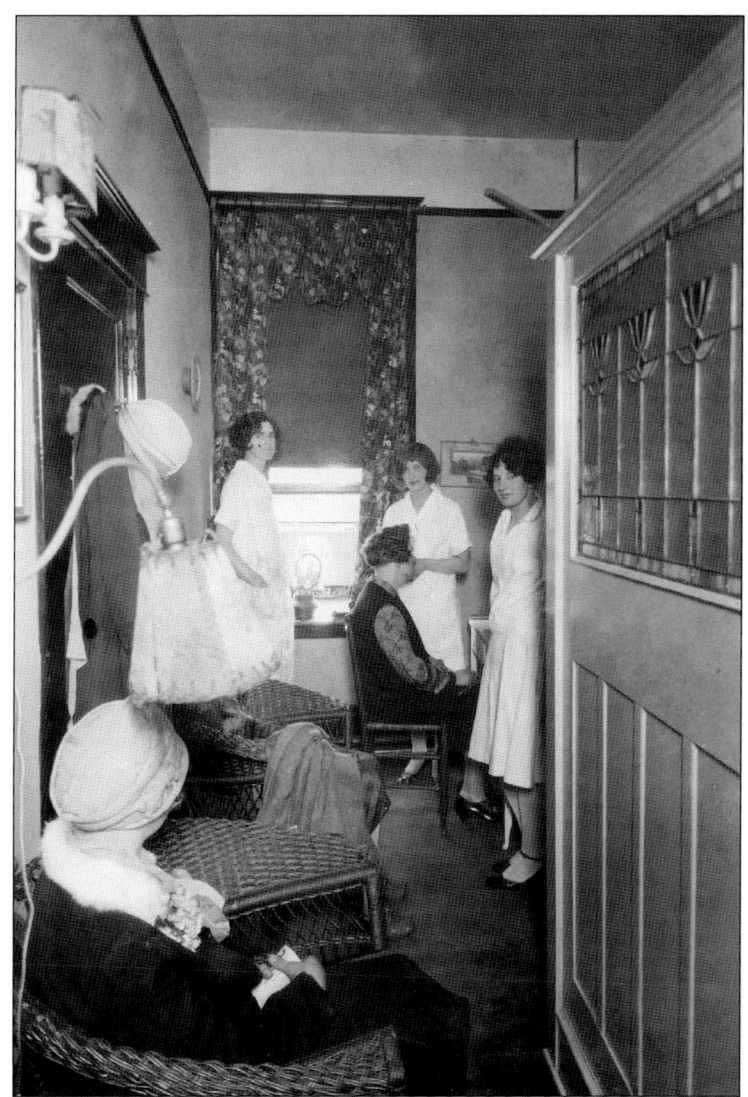

Margaret's Beauty Parlor, circa 1930. The business was located in the McAlpine Building. Included in the group are Margaret Taylor Schultz and Isla Smith.

Transportation

Originally, access to Itasca County was by river. Steamboats, such as the "Irene" and the "Fawn" travelled from Aitkin to the Grand Rapids of the Mississippi, the head of navigation on the Father of Waters.

A major milestone was reached with the arrival of the Duluth and Winnipeg Railroad in 1890, but a lack of good roads made Itasca County a still-remote destination.

County Commissioner Cyrus King, remembered as "the Sage of Deer River", made the development of good roads a major focus of his public service career. Due to the efforts of King and others, as well as state support culminating in the passage of the Babcock "Good Roads" Amendment, Itasca County currently has an excellent system of trunkline highways and tributary roads.

On engine No. 226 are, left to right: Oric Infelt, W.J. McGrath, Noble J. Mason, Ralph Hornbeck, C.T. Peterson, unknown, George P. Durand, Tom Philips, and unknown.

Construction camp of the Duluth and Winnipeg Railroad, which later became the Great Northern, on the banks of the Mississippi at the head of the rapids, May 1890.

Building the railroad west of Grand Rapids, circa 1890.

One method of early transportation in Itasca County was by ox cart, circa 1895.

Early bus from Taconite to Coleraine School, circa 1900.

Steamer "Irene", circa 1902.

Pokegama thoroughfare bridge, 1903.

Engine No. 1 on the M. & R.R. Railroad at Deer River, June 1905. John McVeigh was the engineer.

Building a dam on the thoroughfare between Pokegama and Jay Gould, October 1903.

Steamer "Oriole", 1904. The steamer made regular runs from Aitkin to Grand Rapids.

Frank Myers Dray Line, Grand Rapids, 1906.

Family out for a drive in their Buick near Balsam, circa 1910. Note the ruffed grouse hanging on the side of the car.

A young man picks up a load of Peoples Brewing Co. beer and holds one in hand as he leaves the train, circa 1910.

The steamboat "Irene" between Aitkin and Grand Rapids, 1904. The boat stopped to load wood left by farmers. At the same time they would leave grocery orders for the farmers.

This team of sorrels, "Shorty and Fred," was one of the many fine teams of horses that Charles W. Forrest had on his dray line, circa 1910. Bill Elder has this wagon parked in front of the Thomas Hennessy home on the corner of 1st Avenue West and 5th Street, Grand Rapids.

Joseph Passard's road crew, circa 1910.

Inside the Great Northern Depot, Grand Rapids, 1911. Included are: Joe Stiners, Herry Hicks, and W.G. LeFevere.

Making a big delivery for the Carl J. Eiler store, circa 1912. The advertising on the car door refers to "Carl the Live Grocer".

Grand Rapids depot, 1910.

Group on a Mississippi River wanigan, or cook boat, circa 1910.

John Beckfelt dredge, 1913.

Working on the road near Grand Rapids, circa 1913. From left to right with the rakes and shovels are: R.F. Patten, Frank Reuswig, Joe O'Day, Howard Doran, Judge Webster, Truman Seamans, Art Peterson, Lester Lofberg, and Frank Gumm.

Gentlemen out for a winter's drive in a Brush car, circa 1910. Brush automobiles were made from 1907-1912

Mesaba Transportation Co. bus, one of the first to run from Hibbing to Grand Rapids, circa 1915.

John Lofberg street improvement crew, 1916. They are using the rock crusher and screen in the street north of the Stevens Hotel. The Mississippi River and Powers Hill are in the background.

Building a trestle near Bovey and Coleraine, circa 1920.

The first plane to land on the Coleraine Field in 1928. From left to right are: August Johnson, the pilot; A.E. Nelson, candidate for United States Senator; Alex King; Charles Larson; E. Freemont, and Captain Murphy.

Mrs. Wally Aiken with her car decorated for a special occasion, circa 1920.

Getting ready to build the new Mississippi River bridge, Highway 169, 1933.

Ford tri-motor airplane at the Otis Resort, circa 1930.

Public Service

Strong community spirit was reinforced by dutiful public service. Firemen, police officers, and volunteers all demonstrated a commitment to the common good.

When the call to service has come, Itasca County residents have responded. Businesses were closed and all of Grand Rapids turned out to honor Itasca County men who were preparing to depart for service in the First World War; similar sentiments were observed in other communities as well.

The common good was supported in a variety of ways, ranging from service on juries to the procurement of hospital and library facilities. Such actions helped to make Itasca County less rough around the edges and more conducive to the needs of families.

During the Depression years, numerous Civilian Conservation Corps camps were opened in the forests of Itasca County, and young men were taught valuable skills and earned needed cash while learning the value of public service.

Grand Rapids city officials, circa 1910. Les Burns is second from the right in the back; Ed Martineau is on the right in the front row.

Waldeck Post Office, circa 1890.

St. Benedicts Hospital, Grand Rapids.

Veterans paying respects
to fallen military men
in the cemetery, circa
1900.

Itasca County Courthouse was built and occupied for the first time in 1896.

Grand Rapids Public Library.

Delegates to the Firemen's Convention at Park Rapids, 1900, are, left to right: John Costello, Jesse Harry, William Dibbert, Hugh Shannon, and Joseph Fletcher.

Selective Service Board, circa 1917. Seated, left to right: Judge Keo LeRoux, County Treasurer Frank Sherman, Charles Gunderson, and Dr. Russell. Back row: Jess D. Anthony, Ralph Stone, Dr. Jules Gendron, Dr. Dumas, and Dr. M.M. Hursch.

Petit jurors and officials at the Itasca County Courthouse, 1900.

Grand Rapids firemen, circa 1910.

Itasca County's first contingent of 169 men sent to Camp Dodge, Iowa, September 20, 1917.

Every business in Grand Rapids closed to see their first men leave for the service during World War I, 1917.

Itasca County Hospital, 1918. The women standing on the lawn include Mrs. Shipman and Miss Manthey.

This group was recalled at the close of hostilities on November 11, 1918.

Sheriff's office in the Itasca County Jail, October 1918. Charlie Huss is on the right; Sheriff Ed Carson is behind his desk on the right.

Public officials in the Itasca County Courtroom, circa 1920. Identified are: Royal K. Stokes of Cohasset, County Commisssioner, seated second from the left; Mr. King, standing second from the right; and Mr. Warren, standing third from the right. Mr. Stokes drowned in 1921.

Still taken in 1922 at Deer River by Ed Jess. Also pictured are Ed Carson, Jack Jones, and George Galbreath.

Kitchen at Civilian Conservation Corp. Camp No. 718, circa 1935.

C.C.C. enrollees get practical knowledge of road construction and handling of road building machinery, circa 1935.

Civilian Conservation Camp S-53, Side Lake, circa 1935.

Education

From the beginning, Itasca County citizens placed a high value on education.

Strong and effective leaders were sought for the County's schools. Under "Professor" G.T. Carroll, students at Central School learned Latin and studied Cicero, Caesar, and the classics — unique for a remote northwoods community.

Poor roads made it impossible to transport students to central locations, so rural schools were built throughout the county. The young teachers at these remote locations boarded with local residents and became part of the communities they served. A "Normal School" for teacher training was founded at Central School.

In Deer River, Cyrus King and others established a boarding school so teenagers in rural Itasca County could attend high school. In Coleraine, Greenway High School was built to serve the students of that region. A separate school district was created to meet the needs of Nashwauk and eastern Itasca County.

Classroom at Coleraine High School, 1909.

The first school in Grand Rapids was built in 1888 on the site where Central School later stood. The first building was later moved to Cohasset where it was used as a school and then as a church. Mrs. B.C. Finnegan was the first teacher in the original school.

Grand Rapids School and teachers, 1898. Mr. E.T. Carroll was the Superintendent of School District No. 1. The faculty, from left to right: Hattie Gibson, Lena McCarthy, Elizabeth Sutton, Eliza King, Chink Cleveland, Margaret Doran, Mabel or Bessie Brady, Honore Sutton, and E.T. Carroll.

First public school in Nashwauk, 1903.

First school built in Bovey in 1906 by John Lofberg.

Lawrence Lake schoolhouse, circa 1905.

Central School, circa 1905.

Taconite School.

Chemistry class at the Greenway High School, Coleraine, 1908.

Office of the Greenway High School, Coleraine, 1908. Staff, from left to right: J.A. Vandyke, Ruth Vandyke, and Clarence Bennett.

Coleraine class of 1908. Students are: Flora Gustafson, Luella McArthy, Hazel Prescott, Pearl Trescott, William Fessler, and Ione Stock. J.A. Vandyke was superintendent at that time.

Margaret Aiton's third grade class the first year the Forest Lake School was open, circa 1908.

Students in this early Central School classroom include: L. LaFond, H. Schultz, B. Pearson, Gen Peavey, C. Costello, C. Shannon, Mae Benton, Marg Affleck, I. Flesche, E. Russell, F. Johnson, V. Miller, J. Patell, _ Freeman, _ Murphy, Bill Farrell, Carl Eiler, L. McLaughlin, _ Whibby, L. Audette, Arvida Julland, M. Dahl, E. Quackenbush, _ Weston, and George Vipond.

Deer River school, circa 1910.

Lower Balsam schoolhouse, circa 1910. Alice Hegdahl was their teacher.

Grand Rapids school and students, circa 1910.

School held in the Martin bunkhouse on Trout Lake, circa 1910. Ethel Kremer was teacher to five Martin children and two Haglees.

Bovey School, circa 1910.

Grand Rapids students, 1917. Back row, left to right: Esther Anderson, Thressa Hepfelt, Corinne Beaudry, Ethel Hicks, Margaret Wright, and Bella Rassmussen. Third row: _ Jewell, Lila Maddy, Helen Morris, Pamela LaRoux, Leora Cook, Hazel Clark, and Stella Fritzgerald. Second row: Myrtle Hensel, Alice Gustafson, Mary Buhl, Olymphia La Labertie, Elizabeth La Labertie, Charlotte Hursh, Gertrude Bruck, Eva D'Anjou, and Agnes Eide. Front row: Max Reuswig, David Brandon, Padde Pederson, Millard Lee, and Millard O'Brien.

Central School kindergarten, 1916.

First grade in Grand Rapids, 1912. Students include: Ann Remer, Oliver Sherman, Clarence Lachen, Louis Saure, Elmer Hoolihan, _ Harry, Don Claus, Gene Betts, Hilma Eide, Kenny Parrington, Pearl Patell, Dick Whaling, Alice Arscott, Harold Vipond, Alice Hoey, Emma Bilodeau, Ella Wilcox, Ruth Sheldon, Gertrude Erickson, Wayne Moores, Irene Schultz, and Philip Haper.

Deer River school students and faculty, 1913. Cyrus King was the principal. Sixth from the left is Bertha Breid. Stafford King is reclining in the front.

Grand Rapids High School was built in 1903 on Pokegama Avenue and 8th Street East.

A Grand Rapids classroom, circa 1920.

Wawina classroom, 1924. Students include: Sylvia Nuorala, Aili Lyly, Melia Ainasoja, Saimi Pietila, Tyne Hakala, and Ethel Kauti. Their teacher was Miss Emma Engstrom.

Grand Rapids teachers, circa 1925. Edna J. Murphy is at the right in the top row; Hazel Covert is at the right in the bottom row.

Third grade class, Grand Rapids, circa 1920. Back row, left to right: George Dahl, Kenneth Muller, unknown, unknown, Miss Shemel, Gladys Dinwide, unknown, Syliva Russell, Eunice Kentfield, Paul LaFenier, and Gladys Enebek. Second row: Earney Fuller, Adel Councilman, Mildred Kruger, Flora Erickson, Hazel Jetland, Loraine Trask, Margaret Horton, Esther Johnson, Mary Taylor, June Fredrick, and Alice Libby. Front row: Kermit Stone, unknown, unknown, Shorty Sherman, Al Nygard, unknown, unknown, Carroll Johnson, Larry Thwing, and Loyal Scott.

Sports & Leisure

Itasca County has always been an outdoorsman's paradise. Hunting and fishing, whether for moose and lake trout in the early days or white-tailed deer and walleye today, have comprised an important part of Itasca County culture.

The region's wealth of fish and game led to the opening of numerous resorts, which became an important aspect of Itasca County's economy. Today, hunting and fishing remain as popular as ever, for resident and visitor alike.

Athletics also comprised an important part of life in Itasca County. From municipal baseball teams to competitive high school sports to ski jumping in Coleraine, competitive sports added excitement to life in the northland.

Grand Rapids Juniors baseball team, circa 1918.

Tournament of the Grand Rapids Gun Club, 1899.

Canoeing on Bigfork River, circa 1900.

Cyclists in the early 1900s. From left to right: Roy Bell, Dell Brown, Oscar Mather, Cary Woodruff, Elmer _, Miss Atherton, Miss Lesler, Mr. Baker, Miss Allen, George Booth, Miss Wright, Miss King, and Mr. Budd.

Central High School baseball team, 1902. Front row, left to right: Faye Knox, Henry Ranfranz, unknown, Harry Varley, and Ed Whaling. Back row: Bill Finnegan, unknown, unknown, Bill Hennessy, and unknown.

First Grand Rapids High School football team, 1904.

Successful fishing at Martin's Resort, Trout Lake, 1905.

Off for a grouse hunting day, September 10, 1904. Hunters are: Dan Gunn with his dog "Fan", Ed Kremer, and Bert Powers with his dog "Babs".

Fishermen's camp, circa 1900.

Grand Rapids baseball team, circa 1905. Second row, left to right: Joe Garrets, Jack Stafford, Al Hashey, Louie Jorgenson, and Claude Bell. Third row: John Rellis, Y.W. Huntly, Billy Dibbert, and Joe Fletcher.

Northern Minnesota 1907 Champion football team from Grand Rapids.

Cass Lake versus Grand Rapids, November 1, 1908. Grand Rapids was the winner with a final score of 19-0.

Leroy Wheaton, Dan Gunn, and Bice Martin leaving Martins for Ruby Lake.

Grand Rapids teachers on a wanigan on the Mississippi, 1905.

Bovey baseball team, 1908.

Oliver Mine Co. baseball team, 1909.

A 1909 Grand Rapids football team with some of their fans.

Grand Rapids basketball team, 1911. Back row, left to right: G. Finnegan, Ed Erskine, Carl Hepfel, W. Tyvall, and Fred Carson. Front row: Ralph Brandon, Bill Powers, Tom Erskine, and W.J. Whaling.

Grand Rapids 1909 football team. The players include: Webb Tyndal, Galen Finnegan, John Costello, Bill Powers, Ed Murphy, Howard Reuswig, George O'Brien, Tom Erskine, captain Roy Blood, Ralph Brandon, Henry Graffan, and Walter "Spine" Reuswig.

Grand Rapids baseball team, circa 1910. Team includes: Tom Erskine, _ McMahon, William McAlpine, _ Cotton, Lester Lofberg, Cork Whaling, Bud Betz, Frank McAlpine, Will Powers, Ralph Brandon, and Bus Lee.

Greenway High School football team, Coleraine, 1914.

Boating on Trout Lake north of Wabana, circa 1915.

Grand Rapids Gun Club, 1915. Front row, left to right: Jim Johnson, Jesse Anthony, unknown, and John E. McMahon. Back row: Chet McLaughlin, Art Boardman, Ed Grefe, Frank Sherman, H.D. Powers, Ed Kremer, and Charles T. Kennedy.

Grand Rapids High School Girls Champion basketball team, circa 1915. Players, from left to right: Mary Brandon, Ruth Beckfelt, Gertrude Luther, captain Margaret McAlpine, Miriam Cordes, and Henrietta Kremer.

Bovey baseball team, circa 1910.

Cohasset basketball team, 1917. Back row, left to right: Harry Coleman, Leonard Lambert, and Ray O'Brien. Front row: Charles Metzler, Clarence Parker, and A.C. MeCabe.

Greenway High School basketball team, 1919.

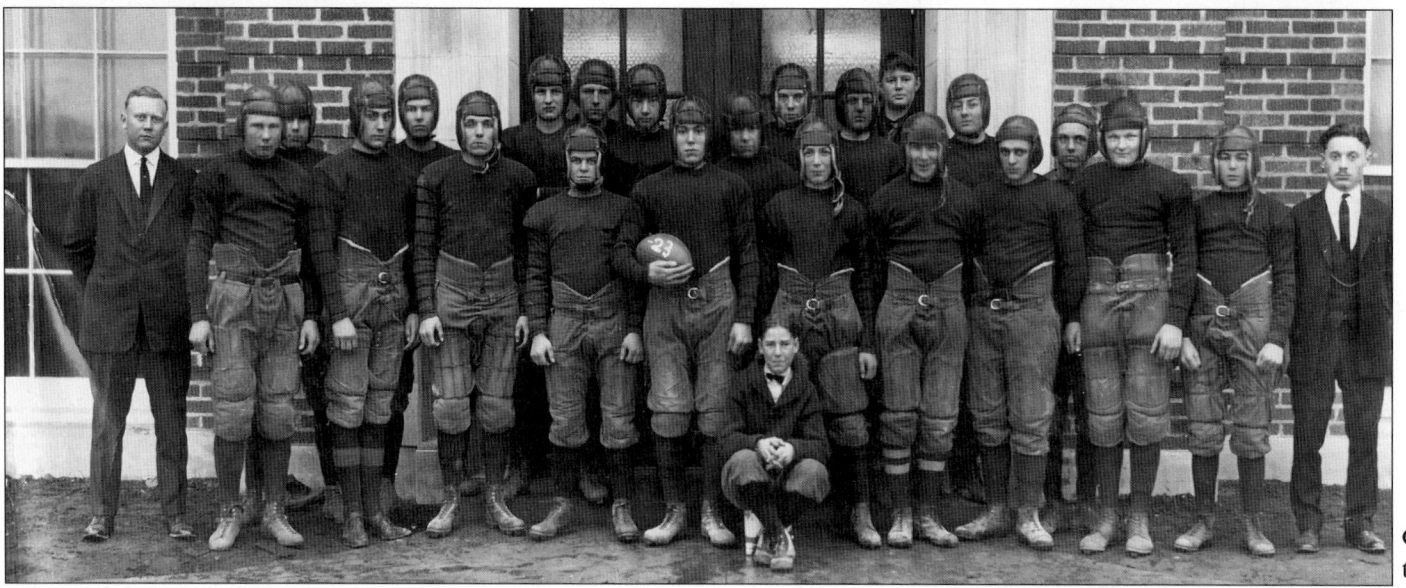

Grand Rapids football team, 1923.

A Coleraine girls athletic team, 1921. Members include: LaVona Jasper, Margaret McGrath, Vivian Franti, and Evelyn Patnaudi.

Grand Rapids city team. They were Mesabi Range Champions, 1922-23. Back row, left to right: Wally Aiken, Hugh Logan, Albert Powell, John Anderson, and Dan Vipond. Front row: Bunny Beaudry, Roger Forest, Sam Lee, __ McDougel, and Leo Miller.

Keewatin hockey team, 1926-27.

Grand Rapids baseball team, circa 1920. Back row, left to right: Bert LaFraniere, Al Wellein, Mordy Winsor, "Sport" Witherill, and George Herrand. Front row: George Blazing, unknown, Lester Lofbert, Stewart McLaughlin, and Fred Beutz. The batboy on the left is Russell McAlpine.

Community

After the dam was built at the foot of Wabana Lake in 1872, lumberjacks were arriving in increasing numbers.

Many moved on but others remained and built communities — homes, schools, and churches.

Itascans exhibit a strong sense of community. Over the years, we have come together to support each other in times of trouble and celebrate with one another in times of joy. We have built institutions and organizations to sustain us.

From Fourth of July celebrations and community festivals having their origin in the opening years of the twentieth century to participation in civic organizations, Itasca County residents have demonstrated a willingness to contribute to the civic and cultural life of the region we call home.

Bovey Boy Scouts, 1928.

Presbyterian Church, Grand Rapids, 1898.

Grand Rapids Catholic Church was built in 1894 and burned on December 30, 1910.

Hotel Pokegama fire, March 23, 1893. The hotel was owned by D.M. Gunn and D.J. Hartley.

A prize load of carrots raised by J. Hendricks, Balsam, circa 1900.

Holum family at their home at 424 3rd Avenue N.E., Grand Rapids, circa 1900. Eilert (Ed) built the house in 1895. He and his wife, Martha, are pictured with their children: Arthur, Edward, Albert, and Dorothy.

A rural Itasca County home, circa 1900. Julie Dahl is on the left.

Effe Durkie and Jarrie Mather peeling apples, circa 1894.

E.J. Farrell with his children in front of their home, 1902. Farrell served as the Itasca County Auditor.

Logging train wreck on a logging road out of Deer River, circa 1907. John McVeigh lost his life in the accident.

Forest fire near Bovey, 1903.

Coleraine City Band, circa 1900.

A Sunday of relaxation at Morris O'Brien's shingle mill at Wellers Speer between Cohasset and Deer River, 1902. Included are: Walt Vail, Gus Monson, Morris O'Brien (in the white shirt and tie in the middle of the front row), Mike Stapleton, Mrs. Monson, Lillian Voss, Martin Brown, Viola Voss, Gertrude Voss, Myrtle Voss, Earl Comstock, Mrs. Earl Comstock, and Mary Stapleton.

First Fourth of July celebration in Deer River, 1906. The Deer Lake float is driven by Doc Parmeter.

Mohr Hotel in Deer River had costumes to rent, circa 1905.

Martin home on Trout Lake, circa 1905. The home burned on March 16, 1906.

John Walberg residence, Balsam, circa 1905.

Mr. And Mrs. William Sandusky and sons, Nashwauk, circa 1905.

John Hoyt's residence, Balsam, circa 1905.

Henry Kannas residence, Balsam, circa 1905.

Ely Rust residence on Prairie River, circa 1910.

Grand Rapids Band on the steps of the Itasca County Courthouse, circa 1905.

Mike McAlpine home, the first frame house in Grand Rapids, circa 1910. Note the family's car parked behind the trees.

Florence Remer, Jeanette Kinney Hog, and Aura Lathrop Trask pose for the camera in 1909.

Grand Rapids women doing their handwork, circa 1910, are, left to right: Rose O'Connell, Mrs. William Powers, Mrs. Wright, and Mrs. Randall Harrison.

Grand Rapids band, circa 1910. Included are: Joe O'Day, Frank Marek, Al Roeker, Charles Oisen, and Bill Nisbet.

This distinguished group of young men, circa 1910, includes: Charles Transin, Franklin McVeigh, Art Cloutier, Budd Betts, _ Shousnessy, and _ Burke.

J.C. Hendricks home built in 1909 was the first frame house in Balsam Township.

Fourth of July celebration at the Frank Bruzewitz place, 1906. Those gathered to celebrate include: Phil Hanck, Lizzie Stempf, Bella Hanck, George Hanck, Anna Robb, Helen Hanck, T. Lefever, Mrs. Lefever, Charlie Schwantez, Chris Stempf, Herman Rieger, Ella Rieger, Old Ziegenfus, E.O. Walley, Jim Meyers, Walter Parson, Frank Bruzwitz, Mrs. Harding, Minnie Stempf, Alex Laracat, Emma Davis, Mr. Davis, _ Brown, and Ed Naylor.

First Farm Bureau meeting in Balsam Township, circa 1910.

A real old-time Grand Rapids orchestra, circa 1910. The man without an instrument is the caller whose name is unknown. The men with instruments, left to right: Charles Aiken, Anton Johnson, Will Nesbitt, and J. O'Leary.

St. Joseph's Catholic Church in Grand Rapids on fire, December 30, 1910.

Crowd gathered in front of Central School for a Decoration Day parade, 1912.

Martin Madson's home on Trout Lake, circa 1910. From left to right: Ole Sherman, Mr. and Mrs. Madson, Einer Johnson, and Axil Johnson.

J.S. Gale residence on 4th Street, Grand Rapids, circa 1910.

Residences near the Crosby Mine, Nashwauk, circa 1910.

C.V. Smith home on Balsam Brook was a landmark for early travelers on the three-day journey between Grand Rapids and Bigfork. It was the largest log structure built in the state at that time for a residence. The home was built in 1907 and is shown here in 1912.

Funeral for the victims of the Calumet catastrophe in which 74 people lost their lives, December 28, 1913.

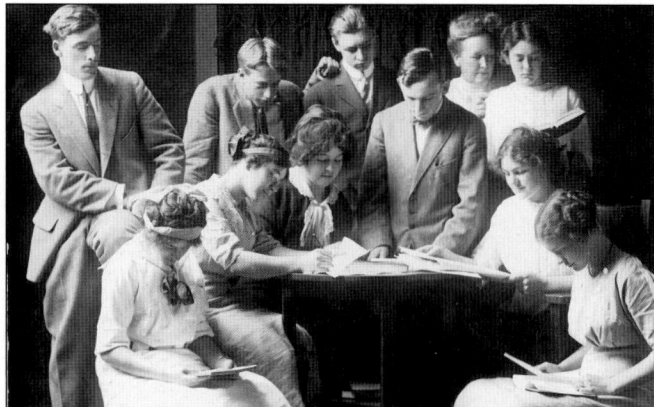

A group of young people in 1913 includes, front row, left to right: Emily Powers, Margaret O'Connell, Muriel Fairbanks, _ Sherman, Eva Staid, and Ethel Kremer. Back row: teacher and sponsor Mr. Carson, Robert Patterson, Rellis Wright, Miss Burlingame, and Bessie Kelley.

Nashwauk High School Band, circa 1913. Eino Rantala is one of the band members.

Farm Bureau picnic on Blue Water Lake at the Wakeman residence, circa 1915.

Coleraine Band, circa 1920.

First professional picture taken of Francis Ethel Gumm (Judy Garland), 1924. She was born on June 10, 1922, in Grand Rapids. Nicknamed "Baby", she changed her name to Judy Garland in 1934, made thirty-two feature films, received an Academy Award, and was nominated for two others. As a singer, she recorded nearly one hundred singles and over a dozen record albums.

The Gumm sisters, 1924. Standing on the left is Virginia; seated is Frances Ethel; and standing on the right is Mary Jane. The sisters performed at theaters around Grand Rapids. Within a few years after the 1926 family move to California, the girls were appearing regularly on local radio shows.

Ethel and Frank Gumm, parents of Virginia, Mary Jane, and Francis Ethel, 1924. When they met about 1913, Ethel was a house pianist for stage performances and silent films and Frank Avent Gumm was a tenor who sang. They formed a duet calling themselves Jack and Virginia Lee, Sweet Southern Singers. They soon got married and toured their show in the upper Midwest before settling in Grand Rapids where Frank managed the New Grand theater. In 1926 the Gumm family moved to Lancaster, California, where Frank bought the local theater and their daughters pursued careers in show business. Ethel was the girls' agent and manager.

Central Kindergarten Band directed by Clara Sinnett, 1923. Included in the first row: Elaine Madson, Wallace Smith, Byron Bentz, Bilson Peterson, Jack Shannon, Bernice Lofberg, Mary Wahlin, Edith Bennett, David Webster, _ Campbell, Gloria Johnston, Ed Shannon, Donald Meyers, and O. McNeeley. Included in the second row: Rosemary Huhn, Vivian Jacobs, _ Montcalm, Captialo Waurms, _ Synder, Virginia Passard, Katherine McAlpine, Peter Golla, Lois Gummerson, and Edith Francis. Included in the third row: Archie Lofberg, David Sheldon, June Scott, Agnes Holm, Kitty Clair Doran, _ Erickson, Dorothy Trainor, _ Vipond, L. Kniffen, and _ Peavey.

Itasca Potato Growers Association, circa 1920. Members include: Ted Alzen, Art Frick, Erik Martenson, O.B. Bendix, and Evald Youngren.

Memorial Day parade in Grand Rapids, 1917.

Bovey parade, circa 1920.

Fire in Bovey, circa 1930.

American Legion Auxiliary band, July 4, 1929. Front row, left to right: Mrs. Ed Jetland, major Margaret Taylor, and Edith Jetland. Second row: Evelyn Knospe, Lorayne Trask, Clara McAffie, Doris Madson, and Inez Madson. Third row: Agnes Smith, Ida Knospie, Charlotte Dorothy, and Pearl McLaughlin. Fourth row: Utah Allen, Ada McClean, unknown, and Mary Huhn. Fifth row: Hilda Schrader, Aura Trask, and Addie Donaldson.

Grand Rapids High School Band, 1930.

Dedication of the Coleraine Airport, July 4, 1929.

Boys Glee Club, Grand Rapids, 1933.

Marble Boy Scout troop, 1939.

Judy Garland returned to Grand Rapids to promote the sale of war bonds in 1937.

Central School Band, 1934, directed by Oscar B. Dahle. Included in the front row: Joan Newburg, Francis Ames, Lillian Bruhn, Margaret Vanderheide, Margaret Ellingson, Bernadine Kranke, Eleanor Bjork, Dorothy Olaniva, and Bob Herendeen. Second row: Duane England, Alvin Grinde, Roger Forrest, Bill Campbell, Marian Olaniva, F. Madson, Ardis Madson, Dorothy Doran, and Kenneth Skattegard. Third row: Audrey Acheson, Corrine Williams, Jean Gildemeister, Betty Snyder, Ellen Birch, Betty Rossiter, Jean Tyndall, Kathryn Hoey, Elberta Erven, Helen Erven, and Marian Sieber. Fourth row: Bill Martineau, Ted Hoolihan, Philip Martineau, Genevive Hachey, Lorraine Brownlee, Ardys Tyndall, Grace Latz, Mary Jo Arens, Patsy Doran, and Kathleen Madson. Fifth row: Ronald Hane, Rolly Boehnlien, Bob Dorothy, Jean Van Calligan, and Fred Bentz.

American Legion annual school patrol police picnic for Central School, Forest Lake. The picnic was held May 11, 1938, at Tyndall Cottage, Pokegama Lake.

The Coles Came to Grand Rapids in 1916

In those days, we worked in the woods, logging and lumbering and did some gardening.

In 1932, Jud, Clair and Alan started the Cole Equipment Co.

The gas station was built in 1935, and we wold trucks, tracotrs, cram separators andother equipment, primarily to farmers in the area.

"THEY SAY COLE'S HAVE IT"

That's been an important slogan for our business since the beginning. We carry extensive inventories of a wide variety of hardware and and other oggs today. If you think what you want is hard to find, come to Cole's first, and see for yourself!

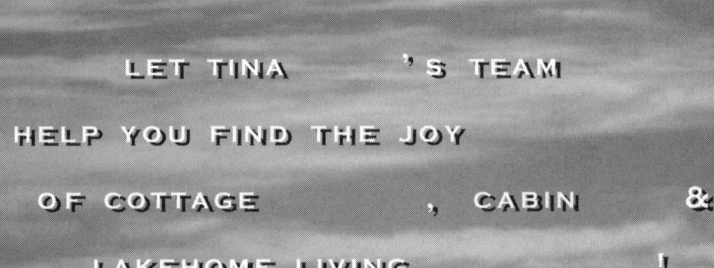